Flavors without Border

A Feast of Indian, Thai, Burmese, and Chinese Delights

Htet Myat Kaung

notionpress
.com

INDIA · SINGAPORE · MALAYSIA

Contents

BURMESE CUISINE

Myanmar Tea Leaf Salad

Serves (2)

- Get a chopping board and a knife, take 2 tomatoes, and slice them into thin slices, remember to remove the seeds from the tomatoes.
- Chop 7 cloves of garlic, 2 chilis, and ⅓ portions of cabbage.
- After you are done chopping, add them into a bowl with the sliced tomato.
- Mix all the ingredients, using a spatula or your hand but don't forget to use gloves. Do not forget to mix the ingredients well.
- Cut a lemon into half and squeeze that half of the lemon into the mixed vegetables that are inside the bowl.
- Add 2 tablespoons of pickled tea leaves. Then add 2 teaspoons of salt and 1 teaspoon of soy sauce, and mix it well.
- Add 3 tablespoons of assorted fried beans, make sure you don't leave the beans outside for too long, or else they will get soggy.
- Mix all the ingredients well and before serving taste if you need salt or anything, after tasting, you can serve.

Ingredients

- Pickled tea leaf
- assorted fried beans
- 2 tomatoes
- 1 Garlic
- 1 Cabbage
- 1 chilli

- 1 bowl of boiled corn
- 1 Lemon
- 2 teaspoon salt
- 1 bowl
- 1 teaspoon of soya sauce

An interesting fact about Lahpet Thoke is its historic role as a peace offering in Myanmar. Traditionally, fermented tea leaves were shared between warring kingdoms to symbolize the resolution of conflicts. This practice highlights the cultural significance of lappet, as it was not only a delicious dish but also a gesture of goodwill and reconciliation. The act of sharing lahpet has evolved into a communal experience, where guests can build their salad from various ingredients, further emphasizing its role in hospitality and social gatherings in Burmese culture.

Shan Noodles

Serve (1)

- Take your garlic and onion and chop them, grind the tomatoes, and after crushing the tomatoes, slice the spring onion, get your chicken slice them into cubes, and keep all the ingredients in different bowls.
- In the chicken bowl add 1 teaspoon of soy sauce and mix it well. Heat your pan and add 2 tablespoons of oil.
- In your heated pan add 2 tablespoons of chopped garlic, and cook the garlic until it is golden brown, after that add onions and mix it well, when the garlic and onion are ready add 1 teaspoon of chili powder.
- Add the sliced chicken to the pan, saute the chicken for 5 to 7 minutes, and add pureed tomatoes, mix, and let it cook for a few minutes.
- When you feel that the tomatoes are cooked add 2 teaspoons of soy sauce, add 1 teaspoon of salt as well, and mix it well. Add ¼ teaspoon of Chinese five spices, pour ½ cup of water into the pan, and let it simmer for 4 to 5 minutes.
- After cooking your tomato paste, add ½ cup of oil to a pan and heat it for 2 minutes, pour the heated oil into a bowl of crushed chili, mix the oil and chili well.
- Heat ½ of oil, add the other chopped garlic, and saute it well, when the garlic turns golden brown add 1 tablespoon of sesame seed, mix it, and keep it in a bowl.
- Finally, take your rice noodles and soak them in the water for 3 to 4 minutes, meanwhile, heat a pot and add water to it add the soaked noodles and boil it for 4 to 5 minutes, remove the noodles and add pea sprouts leaves for another 2 minutes.
- Add sweet soy sauce to your noodle bowl, add 1 teaspoon of soy sauce, pour in the garlic oil that was prepared, and add the chicken curry, add the roasted peanuts and the boiled pea sprouts leaves add the chili oil, on top add 1 teaspoon of salt and mix it then you are ready to serve it.

Ingredients

- 15 to 16 cloves of garlic
- 2 onions
- 2 tomatoes
- Boneless chicken 300 g
- 4 teaspoon oil
- 4 teaspoon soy sauce

- 18 tablespoons of cooking oil
- 1 teaspoon of chilli powder
- 1 teaspoon of salt
- ¼ teaspoon of Chinese 5 spice powder
- ½ cup of water
- 2 tablespoons of crushed chilli

- 1 tablespoon sesame seeds
- 2 to 3 spring onion
- Rice noodles 200 g

- 1 tablespoon of sweet soy sauce
- 3 tablespoons of roasted peanuts
- 2 to 3 pea sprouts leaves

Shan noodles, known as Shan Kauk Swae, are a traditional dish originating from the Shan State in Myanmar. This region is located in the eastern part of the country, bordering China, Laos, and Thailand, which has influenced the culinary practices of the area. Shan noodles are widely enjoyed throughout Myanmar and have gained popularity in neighboring countries due to their unique flavors and simplicity.

Nang ke Toke

Serves (1 to 2)

- Boil the thick rice noodles. Boil it for 2 to 3 minutes Once cooked, drain them and rinse with cold water. Set aside. Mix the peanut oil, fish sauce, lime juice, chili powder, and salt in a bowl. Taste and adjust if needed.
- In a large bowl, mix the cooked noodles with the shredded chicken. Pour the dressing over the noodles and toss everything together until well mixed.
- If you want, sprinkle toasted chickpea flour over the salad and mix gently. Top with fresh coriander leaves before serving. You can enjoy this dish warm or at room temperature. Then you are ready to serve.

Ingredients

- 300 grams of Thick rice noodles
- 200 grams of boiled and shredded Chicken
- 2 tablespoons of Peanut oil
- 2 tablespoons of oil
- 2 tablespoons of Fish sauce

- 2 tablespoons of Lime juice:
- 1 teaspoon of Chili powder
- Salt
- Coriander leaves
- 3 tablespoons of Toasted chickpea flour

Nang Ke Toke, also known as Nan Gyi Thoke (နန်းကြီးသုပ်), is a popular dish in Burmese cuisine, particularly associated with the city of Mandalay. This dish is a thick rice noodle salad with rich flavors and textures, making it a beloved choice for breakfast or as a snack.

Burmese Tomato Curry

- Take the tomatoes wash them and slice them, chop your onions and garlic, and take 3 tablespoons of dry shrimp in a bowl and wash it 3 to 4 times, once done washing soak it.
- Heat your pan and add 1 cup of oil, when your pan is heated add the chopped onions, when the onions are a little red add the chopped garlic, and mix them all until it is golden brown, then 2 teaspoons of Turmeric powder and 2 teaspoons chili powder, mix them all together.
- Add the shrimp paste to the pan, crush it, and mix it to mix the flavors. Add the sliced tomatoes and mix them properly. Drain the soaked dried prawns and add them to the pan, then add 1 teaspoon of fish powder and,1 teaspoon of salt, mix them all, and let it cook for 3 minutes, do not forget to cover the pan, after 3 minutes crush the tomatoes with the spatula and mix it well.
- Add 1 teaspoon of soy sauce, and mix it then add green chill and chopped parsley, mix everything. then you are ready to serve it.

Ingredients

- 8 tomatoes
- 3 onions
- 7 to 8 cloves of garlic
- 3 tablespoons of dry shrimp
- 2 tablespoons of shrimp paste
- 10 green chili
- 1 bunch of parsley

- Oil
- 2 teaspoons Turmeric powder
- 2 teaspoons chilli powder
- 1 teaspoon of fish powder
- 1 teaspoon of salt
- 1 teaspoon of soy sauce

Myanmar tomato curry, often referred to as Nga Sipyan or Burmese Tomato Fish Curry, is a popular dish showcasing Myanmar's rich culinary traditions. This curry typically features fish cooked in a flavorful tomato-based sauce, seasoned with spices such as turmeric, garlic, and chili. The dish is known for its vibrant flavors and is often served with rice, which is a staple in Burmese cuisine.

Burmese Chicken Curry

- Heat the oil and gently fry the chopped onions, garlic, and ginger, until the onions become translucent, add the paprika, turmeric powder, and red chilli paste, and stir in with the fried onions for a minute.
- Add in the chicken, and cook until they becomes white on the outside, add in the water and mix the water with the chicken, let it boil for 3 to 4 minutes.
- Add the fish cause and potatoes and cook the curry for about 10 minutes, add in the coriander and then you are ready to serve it.

Ingredients

- 500g of chicken with bones
- 30 ml of oil
- 1 teaspoon of Perika
- 1 teaspoon of chopped garlic
- 2 chopped onions
- 500ml of water

- 1 teaspoon of crushed ginger
- ½ teaspoon of turmeric powder
- 2 tablespoons of fish sauce
- 1 small bowl of chopped coriander
- 3 potatoes cut into 3-inch cubes
- 5 dry red chilli paste

Burmese chicken curry, known as panthe kaukswe, is a traditional dish from Myanmar that showcases a blend of Indian and Southeast Asian culinary influences. This curry is celebrated for its fragrant spices and rich flavors, making it a popular choice in Burmese households and restaurants.

THAI
CUISINE

Thai Fried Egg

Serves (1)

- Take the frying pan and heat it, let it sit for 20 seconds, add 10 tablespoons of oil and let it sit for 1 to 2 minutes.
- Meanwhile take your egg if the pan is heated, crack open the egg into the frying pan.
- Add 1 teaspoon of salt.
- When the pan is heated add the egg. Let it sit for a bit but make sure that the egg is not burned, after few minutes remove. The egg and you are ready to serve.

Ingredients

- 2 eggs
- 1 teaspoon of salt
- 10 tablespoon oil

Thai Fried Rice

- First prep your ingredients, was your prawns and remove the prawns poop line and wash it thoroughly wash your chicken as well, after cleaning your meats, cut your chicken into 2cm small cubes.
- Take a bunch of springs onions chop it into small pieces chop 4 cloves of garlic, make sure that you have a bowl of steam rice.
- Take your steam rice and add 1 table spoon of soysauce and oyster sauce and mix it and let it sit.
- Heat the frying pan and add 2 tablespoons of oil, heat it for 1 to 2 minutes, after that add your chicken, keep on moving chicken so it does not burn or stick to your pan, add ½ teaspoon of salt to make sure that your chicken has flavor, after making your chicken golden brown remove it and keep it inside a bowl.
- Add your prawns in the same pan and mix it until it is golden brown, remove the prawns once if it is done, keep it in a bowl.
- Add 1 teaspoon of oil if there is less oil, add the chopped garlic and cook the garlic, keep on moving your Spatula until the garlic is gloden brown. Meanwhile take 2 eggs and wisk it in a bowl and add the egg in the pan.
- Mix the egg and garlic add ½ teaspoon of salt and mix it. Add the marinated rice and mix it with the egg, add your fried chicken and fried prawns, mix it well.
- Taste it and check if you want more salt or anything, after that add the chopped springs onion. Then you are ready to serves.

Ingredients

- 5 or 6 prawns
- 1 chicken brest
- 2 table spoon of soy sauce
- 2 table spoon of oyster sauce
- 1 bunch of spring
- 1 bowl of steamed rice.
- 4 garlic cloves

- 2 eggs
- Frying pan
- 2 to 3 bowls
- 2 tablespoon of oil
- ½ teaspoon of paper

Thai fried eggs, particularly known as Kai Dao, are a beloved dish in Thailand, often enjoyed for breakfast or as a side dish. This dish features eggs that are fried until the whites are crispy while keeping the yolk runny. The preparation involves heating a generous amount of vegetable oil in a pan and cracking the eggs directly into the hot oil, allowing the edges to crisp up beautifully. The technique often includes basting the egg whites with hot oil to achieve the desired texture.

Golden Fried Prawns

Serves (2 to 3)

- Start by washing your and remove the prawns poop line, after washing your prawns.
- Marinate your prawns by adding, prawns in a bowl followed by 1 tablespoon of soysauce, 1 tablespoon of salt, 1 tablespoon of garlic and ginger past, mix all ingredients well, cover it and keep it for 15 to 20 minutes.
- Get 3 bowls, in the first bowl crack 2 eggs and wishk it, in the second bowl add⅓ cup of corn starch add 1 teaspoon of paprika, 1 table spoon of salt and mix it. In the third bowl add ⅔ cup bread crumps.
- Take the Marinated prawns and first dip the prawns in the egg and dip it into corn starch, and dip the prawn into the egg again, lastly dip the prawns into breadcrumbs. Repeat the steps with others prawns.
- Heat your chip pan for 2 to 3 minutes, add half liter of oil,add the prawns and let it deep fry for 5 minutes, make sure that you keep on cheeking if it not burned. After 5 minutes if still the prawns are raw or not cooked yet deep fry it for more 2 to 3 minutes Take out the prawns and you are ready to serve it.

Ingredients

- 10 prawns
- 1 table spoon of soysauce
- 2 table spoon of salt
- ⅓ cup of corn starch
- ⅔ cup bread crumbs
- knife
- bowls

- 2 eggs
- 10 ml of buttermilk
- 1 teaspoon of paprika
- garlic and ginger past
- half litre of oil
- chip pan

Thai Golden Fried Prawns, known as Goong Tod, is a popular dish in Thai cuisine characterized by its crispy texture and savory flavor. This dish typically features prawns that are coated in a batter or breadcrumbs and deep-fried until golden brown.

Thai Green Curry

- Minced 6 cloves of garlic and keep it inside a bowl, slice the onions thinly, mince the ginger finely, cut the baby corns into rounds and cut the bell pepper into strips keep all these ingredients in separate bowl, slice the chicken to strips.
- Heat a wok for 5 minutes, add 2 tablespoon of oli, let the oil be heated. Add half of chopped garlic into the wok, saute the garlic for 1 minute, after a minute add the striped chicken into the wok, add ½ teaspoon of pepper and ½ teaspoon of salt.
- Mix it until the color changes and the chicken is cooked, when the chicken is well cooked remove the chicken and keep it in a bowl.
- Add 2 tablespoon of oli in the heated wok, add the sliced onions, saute it until it is translucent, add the other chopped garlic and ginger, mix it for 2 to 3 minutes.
- Open the thai green curry packet, add the paste in the wok, saute it for 3 to 4 minutes, add the cooked chicken, mix it well so that the chicken has the curry flour.
- Add 500 ml of chicken broth and cut kaffir lime leaves into large pieces, **Don't forget to remove before serving**, mix all the ingredients for 1 minutes and let it sit for 2 minutes.
- Add the baby corn and bell pappers cook it for 2 minutes, add 400 ml of coconut milk, mix well in low flame, add 1 teaspoon of brown sugar and 1 tablespoon of fish sauce, add 4 to 5 thai chilli and mix it, last add 7 to 8 thai basil leaves and let it cook for 2 minutes, then you are ready to serve it.

Ingredients

- 1 ready made packet thai green curry
- 300 gms boneless chicken
- 4 tablespoon of oil
- 6 cloves of garlic
- ½ teaspoon of pepper
- ½ teaspoon of salt
- 2 onions
- ½ ginger
- 500 ml chicken broth
- 2 kaffir lime leaves

- ½ cup of baby corn
- ½ cup of bell pepper
- 400 ml of coconut milk
- 1 teaspoon of brown sugar
- 1 teaspoon of fish sauce
- 4 to 5 thai chilli
- 7 to 8 thai basil leaves

Thai Green Curry, known as Gaeng Keow Wan in Thai, is a beloved dish that embodies the rich culinary traditions of Thailand. This curry is characterized by its vibrant green color, which comes from the use of fresh green chilies and a variety of aromatic herbs and spices.

Mango Sticky Rice

Serves (1)

- Get the uncooked glutinous rice, wash the rice a for few time and leave the rice to soak for an hour, after which, drain the excess water.
- Place the rice into a steamer, steam them for 1 hour until the rice is cooked and chewy.
- Heat a pan and add 1 cup of coconut milk, add ¼ cup of sugar, mix it until the sugar is dissolved add ½ teaspoon of salt, mix it well add the steamed rice, mix it and leave it to boil, let tablespoonssorbe some of the liquid, place the rice into a bowl.
- Add ½ cup of coconut milk and 3 tablespoon of sugar, mix it well add cornstarch slurry that contains 1 teaspoon of cornstarch and 2 teaspoon of water, mix it well and leave it to boil.
- Slice the mangoes, now let's plate them. Add the sticky rice in a plate and the sliced mangoes, on top add the sauce and ½ teaspoon of toasted sesame seeds, then you are ready to serve it.

Ingredients

- 1 cup uncooked glutinous rice
- Steamer
- 1 and ½ cup of Coconut milk
- 6 tablespoon of sugar

- ½ teaspoon of salt
- 1 tablespoon of cornstarch
- 2 mangoes
- ½ teaspoon of toasted sesame seeds

Mango sticky rice, known as Khao Niew Mamuang in Thai, is a beloved destablespoonscombines sweet, glutinous rice with ripe mango and rich coconut milk. This dish is particularly popular in Thailand and has become a staple of Southeast Asian cuisine.

CHIN
CUIS

ESE
NE

Chicken and Mushroom Stir Fry

Serve (2)

- Cut the chicken into thin slices and marinate it with soy sauce, 1 tablespoon of cornstarch, 1 teaspoon of sugar, and 2 teaspoons of oil mix it well and set it aside for 15 minutes.
- Slice the onions, and mushroom, mince the garlic and ginger, chop ginger and 2 to 3 garlic cloves, cut spring onions into 2 inches pieces, slice the red chili.
- Add 1 teaspoon of dark soy sauce, 1 tablespoon of soy sauce, 3 tablespoons of oyster sauce, 2 tablespoons of water sugar, and ½ teaspoon of cornstarch, mix the sauce well, until the sugar and cornstarch dissolves
- Heat wok and drizzle oil and stir fry the onions first, then add mushroom and cook just for 1 to 2 minutes, set them aside.
- In the same pan drizzle more oil and add the marinated chicken, let the chicken cook for 2 to 3 minutes, add minced garlic and ginger, mix everything, and cook it for 4 to 5 minutes.
- Pour the sauce inside, add the fried mushrooms and onions back to the wok, and combine everything together, add chili slices and spring onions, then you are ready to serve it.

Ingredients

- 300g of chicken
- 2 tablespoons of soy sauce
- 2 tablespoons of cornstarch
- 2 teaspoons of oil
- 1 big onion
- 100g of white button mushroom
- Ginger

- 3 cloves of garlic
- 2 to 3 spring onions
- 1 red chilli
- 1 tablespoon of dark soy sauce
- 3 tablespoons of oyster sauce
- Water
- 3 tablespoon sugar

Chicken and mushroom stir fry is a popular dish in various Asian cuisines, particularly Chinese. It typically features tender chicken pieces combined with earthy mushrooms and a variety of vegetables, all stir-fried in a flavorful sauce. This dish is not only quick to prepare but also offers a healthy balance of protein and vegetables.

Orange Chicken

- Cut the chicken into 1-inch cubes and keep it aside, in a bow add 1 tablespoon of salt, 1 teaspoon of white pepper, 1 cup of cornstarch, and 3 cups of flour, mix it well and crack an egg into the bowl and add 1 ½ cups of water, add 2 tablespoons of oil and mix it well. Combine the chicken with the batter.
- Keep it aside, heat the pan, and add oil, fry the chicken at least 6 to 7 minutes.
- Mince 2 to 3 cloves of garlic and half of ginger, Heat a pan and add oil, chilli flakes add the garlic and ginger and mix it well add ¼ cup sugar, ¼ cup brown sugar, ¼ cup of orange juice, ¼ cup of vinegar, 2 tablespoon of soy sauce. Combine 2 tablespoon of water and 2 tablespoon of cornstarch and add it into the pan.
- Cook it until it looks like a maple syrup, add the fried chicken into the pan, mix it well and make sure that the sauce is nicely coated to the chicken, on top add 1 teaspoon of sesame oil, and mix it well then you are ready to serve it.

Ingredients

- 900 g of chicken thigh
- 1 tablespoon of salt
- 1 teaspoon of white pepper
- 3 cup of cornstarch
- 3 cups of flour
- 1 egg
- 1 ½ cups of water
- 5 tablespoons of oil

- ¼ teaspoon of chilli flakes
- ½ teaspoon of ginger
- 1 tablespoon of garlic
- ¼ cup of sugar
- ¼ cup of brown sugar
- ¼ cup of orange juice
- ¼ cup of vinegar
- 2 tablespoons of soy sauce

Chinese Orange Chicken is a popular dish in Chinese-American cuisine, characterized by battered and fried chicken pieces coated in a sweet and tangy orange-flavored sauce. The dish exemplifies the fusion of traditional Chinese flavors with American culinary preferences, resulting in a unique and beloved staple often found in Chinese restaurants across the United States.

Chinese Fried Dough

- Get a bowl and add 2 cups of flour, 1 teaspoon of Baking Powder, 1/4 teaspoon of Baking Soda, 1/2 teaspoon of salt, mix it well.
- Crack a egg and add 1 tablespoon of butter, 0.55 cups of cold water, mix into a dough, knead the dough with your hands, cover the dough and let it rest for about 10 minutes.
- After 10 minutes, take the dough to the mat and knead it, knead the dough with your hands and fold it to make it smooth, then roll up the dough and organize it into a rectangle, wrap it and let it rest at room temperature for about 4 hours.
- Sprinkle some flour on it, then. Stretch it out a bit, roll out long strips with rolling pin flattern the edges, cut it into long stripes of about 2.5 - 3 cm width, after cutting, cover it with a plastic wrap to prevent drying.
- Heat a pot and add oil, meanwhile, shape the dough, take a chopstick and dip it in water, draw a line in the middle of the dough sheet, then put another dough sheet on top of this one, then use chopsticks to press it in the middle, and then push it again at both ends to make sure it doesn't break up.
- When the pot is heated, take the dough and hold the ends, and then stretch it to make it longer, put it into the pot. Soon it will float, and when it floats keep turning it to make it swell. Deep fry until golden brown and then you are ready to serve.

Ingredients

- 1 egg
- 1 tablespoon of butter
- Flour: 2 cups all-purpose flour
- Baking Powder 1 teaspoon

- Baking Soda 1/4 teaspoon
- Salt 1/2 teaspoon
- 3/4 cup of cold water 1 teaspoon of Sugar
- Oil

Youtiao (油条), also known as Chinese fried dough or Chinese cruller, is a popular breakfast item in China and various other East and Southeast Asian countries. These long, golden-brown strips of deep-fried wheat flour dough are typically enjoyed with rice congee or soy milk, making them a staple in many households.

Hainanese Chicken Rice

Serves (1)

- Rinse the chicken with cold water and pat it dry. Rub salt all over it. In a large pot, boil water and add ginger and green onions.
- Carefully put the chicken in the boiling water, breast-side up.Once it boils again, lower the heat and cover. Cook for about 30 - 35 minutes until fully cooked. Remove the chicken and put it in a bowl of iced water for about 10 minutes to cool down.
- Rinse the jasmine rice until the water runs clear. In a pot, heat chicken fat or oil and sauté chopped garlic until fragrant. Add the rinsed rice and stir for about 2 minutes. Pour in 4 cups of chicken broth, add salt, and bring to a boil. Cover and simmer on low heat for about 15 minutes until the rice is cooked.
- Blend chilies, ginger, garlic, sesame oil, salt, lime juice, and broth until smooth. Cut the cooled chicken into pieces. Serve the chicken over rice with cucumber slices on the side. Drizzle with ginger - garlic sauce and serve chili sauce on the side. Then you are ready to serve.

Ingredients

- 1 whole chicken
- 4 tablespoon salt
- 12 - 14 cups water
- 4 - 5 slices of ginger
- 2 - 3 green onions
- 3 cups jasmine rice
- 2 ounces chicken fat

- 10 cloves garlic
- Chicken broth
- 3 tablespoons oil
- 3 red chilies
- 1/4 teaspoon sesame oil
- 1/2 teaspoon salt
- 1 tablespoon lime juice

Hainanese chicken rice is a beloved dish originating from Hainan province in southern China, specifically adapted from a traditional dish called Wenchang chicken. This dish consists of poached chicken served with seasoned rice, accompanied by chili sauce and cucumber garnishes. It has gained immense popularity, particularly in Singapore, where it is considered the unofficial national dish and is widely available at hawker centers and restaurants.

Sesame Balls

Serves (2 to 3)

- Pour in some water and 60 g of sugar in a pot, give it a stir and bring it to boil.While waiting prepare the glutinous rice flour add 100 g of flour in a large mixing bowl, once the water has reched to a boiling point and the sugar has dissolved completely, gradually pour into the glutinous rice flour, keep stirring the flour when you are pouring in the water.
- Stir until it forms into a dough, then add in the remaining glutinous rice flour bit by bit, keep on stirring until it doesn't stick to your hands. When the dough has cooled down and it doesn't stick to your hands, knead it with your hands until it's smooth, add 1 teaspoon of oil and knead the dough until everything binds together. When the dough is nice and smooth set it aside and let it rest for 20 minutes.
- Add 100g roasted ground peanuts in a bowl add 4 teaspoon honey, mix until both of them stick together, after mixing shape it into a circle, set it aside until it is ready to be used.
- Dilute some glutinous rice flour in a bowl with some water, mix it and leave it on the side. Take the glutinous rice dough and knead it for a bit and roll it into a cylinder shape to divide into few equal portions.
- Cut the dough with scraper into 2 to 3 inch dough, then shape into a circle, after shaping the dough, place each glutinous rice balls on to your palm flatten it out, press the middle part with your thumb, and place the peanut filling on to it, then seal the glutinous rice balls by twisting the dough upwards, form it into a nice circle again.
- Dip it into the diluted glutinous rice flour then coat it with the sesame seeds, give the ball a good squeeze and shape it inot a nice round circle, set a side and do the same stepst with other balls. Be quick because the dough and dry.
- Once all the balls are coated well with the sesame seeds, heat up 5 tablespoon of oil or any mesure according to you, in a pot when the pot in hot plunge the balls. **DO NOT STIR THEM IMMEDISTELY**, once the oil is bubbling away turn the rice balls around, make sure that the temperature of the oil is not too high or to low. Fry the balls until it turns golden brown color, once they care floating take them out, then you are ready to serve it.

Ingredients

- 155g glutinous rice flor
- 130 ml Water
- 60 g sugar
- 1 teaspoon of oil
- 100g roasted ground peanuts
- 4 teaspoon honey

- 200g sesame seeds
- 5 tablespoon of oil

Sesame Balls, known as Jian Dui in Chinese, are a popular fried pastry made primarily from glutinous rice flour. They are characterized by their crispy exterior coated with sesame seeds and a chewy, often sweet filling, typically made from red bean paste or peanut paste.

INDIAN CUISINE

Bhindi Masala

Serves (2)

- Wash the ladyfinger and cut the tail and the head cut it into 2 inches size.
- Take a pan add 2 tablespoons of oil, add the ladyfingers to the pan, saute them for 3 to 4 minutes, add ½ teaspoon of salt, and mix it well keep the lady finger aside.
- Add 2 tablespoons of oil add Bay leaf, Cardamom, Clove, Cinnamon, and Mace, and mix them add 2 chopped onions, 1 chopped green chili, 2 teaspoons of chopped garlic, and 2 teaspoons of chopped ginger saute the onions till they are nice and brown.
- Take 2 tomatoes and puree them, add the tomato puree in the pan and cook it, add ½ teaspoon of Turmeric powder, 2 teaspoons of chili powder, 1 teaspoon salt,1 teaspoon of cumin powder, and 1 teaspoon Garam masala. Mix it well for 2 minute.
- Take ½ cup of curd, whisk it nicely, add the whisked cured in the pan, mix it nicely, pour 1 cup of water, and mix it well.
- Add the fried ladyfinger to the pan and mix it on top add some chopped coriander leaves and Kasuri methi close the pan and cook it for 10 minutes. Then you are ready to serve it.

Ingredients

- lady finger of 250 grams
- 4 tablespoons of oil
- 2 Onion
- 2 Tomato
- Bay leaf
- Cardamom
- Clove
- Cinnamon
- Mace
- Curd
- Water
- ½ teaspoon of Turmeric powder
- 1 teaspoon Garam masala
- Fresh coriander leaves
- Kasuri methi
- 1 teaspoon cumin powder

Bhindi Masala, also known as Indian Okra Masala, is a popular vegetarian dish in Indian cuisine that highlights the unique texture and flavor of okra (bhindi). This dish is characterized by its semi-dry preparation, where okra is sautéed with a mix of spices, onions, and tomatoes to create a flavorful and aromatic experience.

Mutton Curry Telangana Style

Serves (2)

- Marinate the mutton pieces with the items mentioned. Set aside for 30 mins. Slice the onions & tomatoes. For the masala paste, heat 2 tbsp oil and add all the whole spices. Give a stir and then add the sliced onions. Fry on medium heat for around 5 mins till soft and then add the sliced tomatoes. Also, add 1/4 tsp salt. Mix and fry on medium heat for 3-4 mins till soft. Now add the peeled almonds and mix in for a minute. Switch off the heat and remove it to a plate to cool. Now blend it into a smooth paste.
- Heat oil in a cooker and then add ginger garlic paste. Give a mix & fry on low heat for 2 mins.
- Now add the marinated mutton pieces and sear on high heat for 2 mins. Now add the spice powders, mix, and continue to sear on medium heat for another 5 minutes till the meat is fried and the oil separates.
- Add the masala paste and cook on medium heat for around 10 mins. Reduce heat to a minimum and continue to cook on low heat for another 5 minutes till oil separates, the color of the gravy changes, and becomes a little granular. Now add 400 ml water, give a mix, and pressure cook for 4 whistles. Then you are ready to serve it.

Ingredients

- Mutton - 1 kg
- Salt - 3 tsp
- Turmeric powder - 1 tsp
- Red Chilli Powder - 4 tsp
- Whisked curd/yogurt- 8 tbsp
- Fennel seeds - 4 tsp
- Green cardamom-6
- Cinnamon - 2 small pieces
- Black peppercorns - 1/2 tsp
- Black cardamom - 3 small

- Onions, sliced - 3 medium
- Tomatoes, sliced 3 medium
- Salt - 1/2 tsp
- Soaked & peeled almonds - 20
- Oil - 4 - 5 tbsp
- Red Chilli Powder -1 tsp
- Kashmiri Chilli Powder-4 tsp
- Coriander powder - 3 tsp
- Cumin powder - 1.5 tsp

Telangana-style mutton curry is a beloved dish that reflects the rich culinary heritage of the Telangana region in India. Known for its robust flavors and spicy profile, this dish is a staple in many households, especially during festive occasions and family gatherings.

Aloo Paratha

- Take a bowl, add 2 cups of wheat flour, ½ teaspoon of salt, ½ teaspoon of Carom Seeds, and 1 teaspoon of oil, mix them pour water, and knead the dough. Knead the dough for 10 minutes. Rubb a little bit of oil and make a circle, keep it aside.
- Boil 4 potatoes until they are cooked, when your potatoes are ready peel the skin and mash the potatoes. To the smashed potatoes add 1 teaspoon of Kashmiri red chili powder, ½ teaspoon of garam masala, ½ teaspoon of chaat masala ¼ teaspoon of salt, chopped coriander leaves, and 2 green chills finely chopped.
- Mix the potato stuffing, and keep it aside. Take a little bit of dough, flatten the dough balls, place the allo filling at the center, and seal the dough ball. Flatten the dough ball and keep it aside.
- Heat your pan and place the Paratha on the pan, cook on medium heat on both sides, until golden brown, add some ghee to the Paratha. Once the paratha is nice and golden then you are ready to serve.

Ingredients

- 2 cups of wheat flour
- ½ teaspoon of Carom Seeds
- Water
- 2 teaspoon salt
- 1 teaspoon of oil
- 4 potato

- ½ teaspoon of garam masala
- 1 teaspoon of Kashmiri red chilli powder
- ½ teaspoon of chaat masala
- Chopped coriander leaves
- 2 green chillies

Aloo paratha is a popular Indian dish made of flatbread stuffed with spiced mashed potatoes. The name "aloo paratha" means "potato flatbread" in Hindi, where aloo means potato and paratha refers to the flatbread.

Dal Tadka

- Add ¼ cup of toor dal, ¼ cup moong dal, and ½ cup masoor dal in a bowl and wash it a few times, add the dal to the pressure cooker, pour enough water, add ¼ of turmeric powder and pressure cook for about 5 whistles on medium flame.
- Heat a pan and add 1 teaspoon of oil, 2 teaspoons of ghee,1 teaspoon of Cumin Seeds,2 red chilies, ½ teaspoon of Asafoetida powder, 5 to 6 curry leaves, chopped onions, and chopped green chili mix them all and add chopped ginger, chopped garlic.
- Saute the onions till they are nice and brown then add chopped tomatoes, saute the tomatoes till they get mushy. When your tomatoes are nice and mushy add ¼ teaspoon of turmeric powder, a teaspoon of Kashmiri red chili powder, 2 teaspoons salt, add a few Kasuri methi do not forget to crush them before adding them. Mix everything together and add the cooked dal.
- Mix the dal well, then add ½ half a cup of water, and mix it well let it cook for 15 minutes. After 15 minutes add ½ teaspoon of garam masala and Chopped coriander leaves, mix it, and then you are ready to serve it.

Ingredients

- ¼ cup of toor dal
- ¼ cup moong dal
- ½ cup masoor dal
- Water
- 1 teaspoon of turmeric powder
- 2 teaspoons of ghee
- 1 teaspoon of oil
- 1 teaspoon of Cumin Seeds
- 2 red chili
- ½ teaspoon of Asafoetida powder
- 5 to 6 curry leaves

- 2 chopped onions
- 2 chopped green chili
- 1 teaspoon chopped garlic
- 1 teaspoon chopped ginger
- 2 chopped tomatoes
- 2 teaspoons of Kashmiri red chilli powder
- 2 teaspoons of salt
- Kasuri methi
- ½ teaspoon of garam masala
- Chopped coriander leaves

Dal Tadka is a beloved dish in Indian cuisine, known for its comforting flavors and versatility. It primarily consists of lentils, typically yellow lentils like moong dal or toor dal, which are cooked and then enhanced with a tempering (tadka) of spices.

Chicken Tikka Masala

Serves (2 to 3)

- Place 500 g of boneless chicken, add 2 teaspoons of ginger and garlic paste, 4 teaspoons of Kashmiri chili, ½ teaspoon of garam masala, 1 teaspoon of salt, add 4 tablespoons curd, 2 teaspoons of lemon juice, 2 tablespoons of oil. Mix all the ingredients together, add a small bowl of hot charcoal add Ghee to it, and cover it for an hour.
- Heat oil in a frying pan and place the tikkas side by side. Don't crowd the pan, you can do it in batches. Fry on medium heat for 2 mins and then turn on the other side. Continue to fry it on medium heat on the other side for another 2 minutes. Now turn it again and continue to fry it on low heat for 3 mins. Flip it and continue the same on the other side too. Take these out on a plate and repeat with the balance of marinated tikkas.
- Heat 2 tbsp oil in a pan and add the chopped onions. Fry on medium heat for 5 mins till light brown in color. Add the ginger garlic paste and fry on low heat for 2 mins Add the tomato puree, give a mix, and add the turmeric, red chili, coriander, cumin powders, and a pinch of salt. Mix & fry for 2 mins on low heat.
- Add the fried tikkas, give a mix, and add 300 ml water. Add the garam masala powder, give a mix and cover & cook on low heat for 10 mins. Now open the lid, add the cream, give a mix, and cook on low heat for 2 mins Lastly add the roasted & crushed Kasuri Methi and cook on low heat for 2 mins. then you are ready to serve it.

Ingredients

- 500g of boneless chicken
- 4 tablespoon curd
- 2 teaspoons of lemon juice
- 4 teaspoons of Kashmiri chilli
- 1 teaspoon of garam masala
- 1 teaspoon of salt
- 4 tablespoons of oil
- 1 teaspoon of turmeric powder
- 2 chopped onions

- 4 teaspoons of ginger and garlic paste
- 2 tomato puree
- 6 tablespoon of cream
- 1 teaspoon of red chilli powder
- 1 teaspoon of Coriander Powder
- ½ teaspoon of Cumin Powder
- 1 tablespoon of Kasuri Methi
- A small bowl of charcoal
- Salt - 1 t

Chicken tikka masala is a renowned dish that embodies a fusion of Indian and British culinary traditions. It consists of marinated boneless chicken pieces, traditionally cooked in a tandoor (a cylindrical clay oven), and served in a rich, creamy tomato-based sauce seasoned with various spices. This dish is celebrated for its complex flavors and vibrant colors, making it a favorite among curry enthusiasts worldwide.

www.ingramcontent.com/pod-product-compliance
Ingram Content Group UK Ltd.
Pitfield, Milton Keynes, MK11 3LW, UK
UKHW051144230225
455404UK00020B/11